I've Been Writing A Newspaper Column For So Long I Don't Think I Could Hold A Real Job Anymore

The Wit And Wisdom Of

Joe Kelly

all the best,

Illustrations by *Kelly - 1996-*

Randall Kimberly

Good Times Publishing Company
P. O. Box 4545
Utica, NY 13504

I've Been Writing A Newspaper Column For So Long I Don't Think I Could Hold A Real Job Anymore

The Wit And Wisdom Of
Joe Kelly

Grateful acknowledgment is made to the Observer-Dispatch for permission to reprint excerpts from columns.

Library of Congress Cataloging-in-Publication Data

Kelly, Joe, 1946-
I've been writing a newspaper column for so long I don't think I could hold a real job anymore: The Wit and Wisdom of Joe Kelly / Illustrations by Randall Kimberly.
p. cm.
ISBN 0-9639290-4-6
I. Title
PN4874.K416K45 1995
818'.5402--dc20 95-43574
CIP

Printed in Oneida County, New York

Also By Joe Kelly

Utica Sesquicentennial Scrapbook

*Joe Kelly's
Greatest Ever Little Trivia Book*

*The Train Doesn't Stop In
Wagner, Montana
Anymore And Neither Do I*

This book is dedicated to:

Bob Wood
Earle Reed
Al Pylman
Dick Jordan
Frank Williams
Dusty Wood
Chuck Tillson

Team Sara

And to the thousands of people who supported us on our bike ride to Washington, D.C., a trip made to call attention to the plight of missing children.

.

A Few Words

I've never met Garry Purcell of Deansboro, but I know we have at least one thing in common. We both like to have fun with words.

Purcell sent me a letter in which he coined a new word: Kellumn. That, Purcell said, is what you call a newspaper column written by Joe Kelly.

I don't think "Kellumn" will catch on, but I appreciate Purcell thinking of me.

Having fun with words is what this book is about. Some serious thoughts are mixed in, though. I'll leave it to you to decide which is supposed to be funny and which is serious.

I'm fortunate. I receive about 100 letters a week from people such as Garry Purcell. They send me ideas, advice, criticism and jokes, jokes such as this one:

A man comes home to find his wife in bed with another man. With raging anger in his voice the husband shouts, "What the hell are you doing?"

His wife looks at him with disgust and then turns to the man in her bed and says, "Didn't I tell you he was stupid?"

A grandmother sent me that one.

Many people send me jokes not suitable for a family newspaper. Since this isn't a family newspaper, I'll tell one of them.

"I've got problems with my marriage," a senior citizen wrote in a letter to Dear Abby. "My first husband passed away and I recently remarried. My new husband is nearing 80 years old, but all he thinks about is sex. He won't let me rest. It doesn't matter where I am or what I'm doing, he comes after me for sex. He has tried to have sex with me while I was washing dishes and cooking dinner. He even tried something while I was bending over to get the clothes out of the washer. Any suggestions on what I can do?

P.S. Please excuse the jerky handwriting."

People also send me ethnic jokes. You can't tell an ethnic joke in a newspaper these days. People are too sensitive and newspapers are very politically correct.

Say something about the Irish and drinking and the Friendly Sons of St. Patrick will get upset. Mention that Italians talk with their hands and the Sons of Italy will get mad. Mention that the Scotch are tight with a dollar and you'll get angry letters.

Which reminds me.

After living in the United States for 10 years, a man returned home to his native Scotland. He was greeted at the front door of the family homestead by his brother, who had a beard down to his knees. The returning brother asked, "Why the beard?"

His brother responded, "When you left you took the razor with you."

Gypsies are the only group you can poke fun at without getting too many people upset. So I will.

"Have you ever flown Gypsy Airlines? It has the lowest fares in the country, but when you land your wallet will be gone."

If you have gypsy blood running through your veins, please don't send me an angry letter.

I can't keep up with my mail as it is.

Thousands of people have written me over the years. Many of those letters - I'm sorry to report - haven't been answered. All have been read, though, and 99 percent of them have been appreciated and enjoyed.

Not answering mail bothers me tremendously. Anyone who takes the time to write deserves an answer. It became impossible for me to do that years ago. Letters come in at about 100 a week, every week. That's no excuse, though, for not answering.

I remember a speech I gave a long time ago. When it was finished, I was asked to answer a few questions.

This was the first question: "I wrote you a letter," a woman in the audience said, "but you never responded."

I explained that I received a lot of mail and was having trouble answering it all.

She said, "I sent Mike Royko (the syndicated columnist) a letter and he responded right away. And he gets a lot more mail than you."

Which is true. He also has a staff who answers his mail.

Letters from O-D readers have proven to be a popular part of my column. I use excerpts from those letters for my monthly mailbag column. People tell me they enjoy my quick-witted responses. Sometimes it only takes me an hour or two to come up with a quick-witted answer.

Some of those letters are included here.

As for the quotes in this book, they come from speeches I've given, lectures at Utica College and Mohawk Valley Community College, my WIBX talk show, personal and business correspondence and, of course, the newspaper column I've been writing since 1984.

I wish I had a list of the people who have been nice enough to send me a joke, who have taken the time to tell me a story, or who have provided the inspiration for the quotes you are about to read. I would like to publicly thank them.

On second thought, that wouldn't be possible. The list would be too long.

I've enjoyed putting this book together. I hope you enjoy reading it.

Joe Kelly

On former Oneida County Executive Bill Bryant:
He didn't like me, which made us even.

On writing a daily newspaper column:
The good thing about writing a column is that it doesn't involve heavy lifting and your hands don't get dirty.

I don't make mistakes. There have been times, though, when my fingers hit the wrong keys.

Editors are a necessary evil. If we could put out a newspaper without them, I'd be all for it. The trouble is that we can't.

-<●>-

On Gil Smith, retired executive editor of the Observer-Dispatch:
He was a tough boss and a great editor. Why he took a chance and hired me in 1976, I'll never understand.

-<●>-

On Gil Smith, retired executive editor of the Observer-Dispatch:
I quit the O-D, went to work for a newspaper in Arizona, didn't like it, wanted my old job back, and Gil hired me again. He's a tough boss and a great editor. He doesn't learn from his mistakes, though.

-<●>-

-<●>-

It's easy for reporters to tell when they've covered a controversial subject fairly. Both sides are yelling at them.

-<●>-

On the Observer-Dispatch:
We're in the communications business. Within seconds of something happening anywhere in the world, we know about it in the newsroom. Sometimes, though, we have problems communicating with each other.

-<●>-

-<●>-

I love lawyers, boxing promoters and politicians. Thanks to them, journalism is only the fourth most disliked profession in the country.

-<●>-

I'm not interested in leaving the O-D, but I'm not sure why.

-<●>-

Most successful writers were geeks in high school. Why this is, I don't know. But it's true.

-<●>-

-<●>-

I don't have to worry about facts. I'm a newspaper columnist.

-<●>-

I can understand why artists would paint for nothing and why musicians would play for nothing but any writer who would write for nothing is stupid.

-<●>-

There's something about writing which makes people agreeable to doing it for free. That keeps the salary low for those of us who insist on being paid.

-<●>-

A good reporter doesn't necessarily make a good editor. I know of several examples.

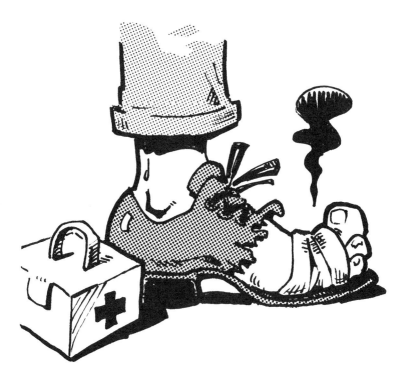

Newspaper columns are like a loaded gun. If you aren't careful with it, you'll shoot yourself in the foot.

-<●>-

The better the writer, the more trouble he or she has writing. People who don't have any trouble writing usually aren't very good writers.

-<●>-

When I'm reading I don't want to have to reach for a dictionary. The same thing is true when I'm writing.

-<●>-

If you write enough columns, sooner or later you'll put together a good one. The law of averages is on your side. That's why I write a daily column.

-<●>-

-<●>-

The sound of a politician saying "I'll cut taxes," and "I'll bring more jobs to our area," and "I'll cut waste" is like the sound of a baseball being hit with an aluminum bat. It doesn't ring true.

-<●>-

On walking 135 miles from Washington Mills to Rochester with Bob Wood to support the parents of Kali Poulton, a missing child:
It was easy. All I did was get behind Bob and follow.

-<●>-

I once had a mayor tell me that getting elected was based one third on hard work, one third on personal image, one third on the issues and one third on luck. He was a good mayor, but his math skills weren't so hot.

-<●>-

Politicians and writers are interesting people but I don't enjoy hanging around with either one of them. I'd rather be with normal people.

-<●>-

Politicians are human, but so are embezzlers, boxing promoters and horse thieves.

-<●>-

I hate it everytime the Uptown Grill wins the "best fish fry in town" contest. The Friday night line is already too long.

-<●>-

-<●>-

Kewpee hamburgers are excellent hamburgers and they taste even better because you can't get them in New York anymore. The tougher something is to get, the more you want it.

-<●>-

-<●>-

If I was rich, I wouldn't write. I'd go sit somewhere in the sun and read what writers who need money had to say.

-<●>-

I can remember every column I've ever written, which is too bad. There are several I'd give anything to forget.

-<●>-

It's hard to write a column that's easy to read.

-<●>-

-<●>-

There are some people in my profession who make me want to leave my profession. There are people like that in every profession, every trade, every line of work.

-<●>-

On Al Neuharth's autobiography, <u>Confessions of an S.O.B.</u>:
At least he got the title right.

-<●>-

-<●>-

On mystery writer John D. MacDonald, who grew up in Utica:
The thing that impresses me is that he had so many people telling him he had no writing talent but he kept at it and eventually became a great success. I would have given up. I think most people would have given up. That's what separates great ones from the rest of us.

-<●>-

On the rigors of writing a newspaper column:
I can't complain too much. I only have to write a column on days that have a "d" in them.

-<●>-

-<●>-

Knowing a great deal about journalism makes me skeptical of things I read in the newspaper, hear on the radio or see on TV.

-<●>-

Anyone can call themselves a writer. The trick is getting somebody to pay you. Then you're really a writer.

-<●>-

Answers to all the questions are in the Utica Public Library. The trick is finding the right books to look in.

-<●>-

-<●>-

Hosting a live radio talk show is a lot like landing an airplane. If you can walk away after it's finished, you've been successful.

-<●>-

After listening to John Swann do his talk show so easily for so many years, I figured I wouldn't have any problem. Then I got my own show and found out that I'm no John Swann.

-<●>-

There's nothing wrong with Utica that a good mayor couldn't fix.

On whether Utica is ready for its first female mayor:
She couldn't do any worse than the men.

Funny thing about humor, no matter what the subject of the joke, at least 10 people will get mad. If I stay at this job long enough, I'll have everybody in town upset.

-<●>-

The two most difficult things for a writer is to get people to laugh and to cry. Of the two, getting laughs is toughest.

-<●>-

-<●>-

On whether there's a secret to keeping up with writing a daily newspaper column and hosting a daily radio talk show:
Yes, it's called daily prayer.

-<●>-

I take my job seriously, but I don't take myself seriously.

-<●>-

On the Kenyans and other world class athletes who have run the Boilermaker: They didn't seem worried about having me in the race.

-<●>-

Only two words are needed to explain the Boilermaker's success: Earle Reed.

-<●>-

If running the Boilermaker was easy, everybody would do it.

-<●>-

I wonder if the reason why so many people run the Boilermaker has anything to do with the fact that the finish line is at a brewery.

Oftentimes when someone asks me to stand up I already am.

-<●>-

I have limitless limitations.

-<●>-

Working at a newspaper is always fun, always exciting, very lucrative and my name is Prince Charles.

-<●>-

My golf game isn't all that bad. In fact, I hit the woods quite nicely. My problem is finding the ball in there.

-<●>-

If you write for a newspaper long enough, you'll get just about everybody mad at you.

-<●>-

Part of my job as a newspaper columnist is to be humorous. I take that very seriously.

-<●>-

On the walk to Rochester with Bob Wood:
I wouldn't have missed it for the world, but I'm glad we don't have to do it again.

-<●>-

There are 10 rules that guarantee a successful career as a newspaper columnist. Unfortunately, nobody has ever told me what they are.

-<●>-

-<●>-

I've given several commencement speeches. The first was at Brookfield Central School. I learned two important lessons there.

The first lesson had to do with humility.

Brookfield is a small district and there were only a handful of graduating seniors. I was surprised when I pulled into the school's parking lot and saw it filled with cars. I looked inside the gymnasium. It was packed with spectators.

I was pleased and proud that so many people had turned out to hear me speak, especially since it was such a beautiful Saturday evening.

As the processional marched into the gym I turned to the school superintendent walking next to me and said how pleased I was to see hundreds of people in the gym.

"With such a small senior class, I didn't think we'd have more than 50 people here," I said. "There must be 10 times that many."

The superintendent looked at me and said, "We always get this many people for our commencement."

"How's that possible?" I asked. "This is such a small school."

Said the superintendent, "On a Saturday night in Brookfield there isn't anything else to do."

Lesson number two had to do with speechmaking.

Before we marched into the gym that evening, I was introduced to each of the graduating seniors. The last one I shook hands with was a 17-year-old farm boy.

"Mr. Kelly," he asked, "have you ever given a commencement speech before?"

"This will be my first," I replied.

"Have you been to Brookfield before?" he asked.

"This is my first time."

"Would you like three words of advice guaranteed to make your speech here a success?"

"Of course I would. What are the three words?"

He looked me in the eye and said, "Keep it short."

I did and I was a success.

-<●>-

-<●>-

There are 11 pages of lawyers listed in Utica's Yellow Pages. There are less than two pages of plumbers, which proves something I've always known. We need more plumbers and less lawyers.

-<●>-

Jim Donovan was a hard worker. Every now and then he would put in a 12 hour work day. The rest of the time he worked 16 hours a day.

-<●>-

Say what you want about Jim Donovan's politics or his personality or anything else. Just don't ever say he wasn't a hard worker. He worked morning til night. He wasn't the smartest or most educated New York State senator, but he was the hardest working.

-<●>-

Every morning my routine is the same. I get up, go to the door, get the newspaper and check the winning Lottery number. If my number isn't there, I go to work.

-<●>-

There's an old journalistic tradition that is responsible for getting me to where I am today. It's called "sucking up to the boss."

-<●>-

I don't intend to grow up. If I did, they wouldn't let me be a columnist anymore.

-<●>-

-<●>-

The following words can be found in Webster's Dictionary, but not the following definitions:

Moccasin - Making fun of evil.

Microwave - A tiny swell of water.

Begun - Used for shooting honey-loving insects.

UCLA - What you see when you go to California.

Intent - Where you put your sleeping bag when camping out.

Paralyze - Two fibs.

Urine - Opposite of "you're out."

Plastic Sturgeon - A fish doctor.

Cauterize - Making eye contact with a woman.

Rescind - Sinning once and then sinning again.

Minimum - A petite English mother.

Terminally ill - Getting sick at airports.

Paradox - Two doctors.

Racist - Someone on the NASCAR circuit.

-<●>-

-<●>-

There are three things every kid should do upon entering college: Convince their parents to give them a credit card, buy lots of underwear, and find someone smarter than themselves to date.

-<●>-

There are basically two kinds of people in this world: those who pull off Band-Aids very slowly and those who take them off in one brutal yank.

-<●>-

-<●>-

There are some newspaper editors who tell you how to write the story before you've even gone out and gathered the facts.

-<●>-

Observer-Dispatch reporters are quick to help TV and radio reporters. They don't care who gets the story first - as long as it's somebody employed by the Observer-Dispatch.

-<●>-

Frank Tomaino is the best city editor I've ever had. I ought to know. I've seen enough of them come and go.

-<●>-

-<●>-

I love country music. In fact, I collect country song titles. Say what you want about country music, just don't ever say they don't have catchy titles.

These are some of my favorites:

"It Ain't Easy Bein' Easy"

"Heaven's Just Sin Away"

"Your Name May Be Chardonnay (But There's Moonshine in Your Eyes)"

"We Need to Put a Little Love Back in Our Sex Life"

"If Today Was a Fish, I'd Throw it Back In"

"I'm So Miserable Without You, It's Almost Like Having You Here."

"He's Got a Way With Women and He Just Got Away With Mine."

"I'd Lie to Get Your Love and That's the Truth."

"I Woke Up on the Right Side of the Wrong Bed This Morning."

"Get Your Biscuits in the Oven and Your Buns in Bed."

"You're Gonna Ruin My Bad Reputation."

"I'm Having Daydreams About Night Things in the Middle of the Afternoon."

"You're So Good When You're Bad."

"You Two-Timed Me One Time Too Often"

"Sleeping Single in a Double Bed"

"I Don't Mind the Thorns (If You're the Rose)"

"If I Said You Have a Beautiful Body Would You Hold It Against Me?"

-<●>-

-<●>-

Not many people know this but I'm a frustrated song writer. I've even come up with great titles for country songs.

These are some of them:

"Baby, Your Generation Gap is Showing"

"Your Hourglass Figure Has Disappeared Into the Bottom of the Glass"

"You Take Me Up and Down Like a Window Shade"

"After I'm Home With You For a Day or Two I'm Ready to Get Back on the Road"

"You Make Me Feel Like a Newspaper on the Bottom of a Bird Cage"

"I Wish I Had Signed Our Marriage License With Invisible Ink"

"A Bad Night of Country Music is Better Than a Good Day at Work"

"I Wish He Was More Like Santa - Stay a Few Minutes and Be Gone"

"I Always Remember a Face But I'm Makin' an Exception With You"

"The Nicest Thing I Can Say About You Isn't Very Nice"

"If Being Stupid Was Against the Law, You'd Be Serving a Life Sentence"

"Seeing You Again Reminds Me Why I've Stayed Single So Long"

"I Don't Deserve Your Love, Baby, But I've Got a Cold and I Don't Deserve That, Either"

Now all I have to do is write the lyrics.

-<•>-

-<●>-

Some people have been kind enough to say that my column alone is worth the price of the newspaper. They've got it wrong, though. They pay 50 cents for the news, sports, comics, weather and stock prices. I get thrown in for free.

Other people have said my column is terrible. What do they expect for something they get for free?

-<●>-

When I was a baby, I was dropped on my head. My mother swears there was no damage, but I've always wondered. It would explain a lot of things I've done as an adult.

-<●>-

-<●>-

What people don't understand is that I'm working even when my hands are clasped behind my neck and my feet are up on the desk and my eyes are closed.   Now if I'm snoring, that's another matter.

-<●>-

I've known two perfect people in my life. I didn't like either one of them.

I love being a newspaper columnist. I get my picture in the paper, and every now and then somebody even buys me a beer. The problem is having to write a column five times a week.

I don't think I have any enemies, but I have a couple of friends who don't like me very much.

Sometimes I don't rewrite my column. Sometimes I rewrite it dozens of times. You can tell which are which.

Not all newspaper reporters are writers, no more than all cooks are chefs.

-<●>-

When I feel myself getting too big for my britches, I remember what basketball coach Bobby Knight once said: "All of us learn to write in the second grade. Most of us go on to greater things."

-<●>-

I hate it when hateful people hate me for hating hateful things.

-<●>-

Having one of my clippings attached to someone's refrigerator door is the ultimate compliment. Whenever I go into someone's home I always check out the refrigerator.

-<●>-

-<●>-

I could say nice things about the people running government, but I'd rather tell the truth.

-<●>-

If baloney was snow, Mario Cuomo would be a blizzard.

-<●>-

I get all sorts of interesting mail. I once opened an envelope to find nothing but a dollar bill inside.

On one side of the dollar was printed this message: "How do you keep a newspaper writer busy? (See other side)"

I turned the bill over. On the other side was this message: "How do you keep a newspaper writer busy? (See other side)"

I didn't write a column that day. I was too busy.

-<●>-

-<●>-

I would never run for office. I'm not smart enough and I don't know anything about politics or leadership. Unfortunately that hasn't stopped others from running.

-<●>-

I attend a lot of meetings, but I've never attended one that ended too soon.

-<●>-

Golf is a good game. I wish I didn't play it so badly, though. At least I hear some good stories out on the course.

Sam, 45 years old and balding, married a beautiful 22-year-old redhead. Before they left on their honeymoon, he took her aside and said he wanted to be completely honest.

"Look," he said, "I have a confession to make. Golf is the most important thing in my life. I eat golf, sleep golf, dream golf. Golf is all I ever think about.

She replied, "Well, honey, I also have a confession to make. I'm a hooker."

"That's no problem," Sam said as he grabbed her wrists. "I can correct that. If you hold your left hand over your right hand like this...."

-<●>-

I don't believe in superstitions. People who do have bad luck.

-<●>-

-<●>-

I wasn't driven into the newspaper business by any great desire to change the world or to do good for mankind. I just didn't want to work in a factory.

-<●>-

The Observer-Dispatch, and every other daily newspaper, is a multi-million dollar operation, which ends up being dependent on a 12-year-old delivery kid.

-<●>-

I've worked at the Observer-Dispatch for nearly 20 years. It's just beginning to dawn on me that I'm never going to be the publisher.

-<●>-

-<•>-

Nothing is easy and everything is more difficult than it looks. Believe that and you'll never be surprised.

The more you write the easier it is to write. The less you write the tougher it gets.

-<•>-

-<●>-

If something can be imagined, it can be made real. I imagine a world without lawyers.

-<●>-

I don't mind climbing a high ladder as long as I know the person holding the bottom.

-<●>-

Just as there is no such thing as a "secret," there is no such thing as "off the record."

-<●>-

Whatever a Utica mayor does, someone will think it's wrong.

-<●>-

-<●>-

Money doesn't grow on trees, but if it did, all mine would come down with Dutch Elm Disease.

-<●>-

Every man has at least one great idea for a business that won't succeed if tried.

-<●>-

The worst thing about flying from Syracuse to New York City on USAir is that there is barely enough time for a beer.

-<●>-

If you find a running shoe that's perfect, buy as many pair as you can afford because they are going to stop making that model next year.

-<●>-

It isn't an accident that "flog" is "golf" spelled backward.

-<●>-

Hosting a radio talk show is a hard way to make an easy buck.

-<●>-

-<●>-

I never watch myself on television, look at my picture in the newspaper or listen to my voice on the radio. Anybody who looked and sounded like me would do the same.

-<●>-

The reason I never use any big words in my column is because I don't know any.

-<●>-

How's business?

I'm glad you asked.

Said the astronomer:
"Things are looking up."

Said the deep-sea diver:
"I'm going under."

Said the photographer:
"It's developing."

Said the baker:
"I'm making dough."

Said the tailor:
"Sew-sew."

Said the sailor:
>**"Knot bad."**

Said the weather forecaster:
>**"Dark and gloomy."**

Said the air-conditioning repairman:
>**"Not so hot."**

Said the garbage man:
>**"Things are picking up."**

Said the fire truck driver:
>**"I'm always in the red."**

Said the mortician:
>**"Things are dead."**

-<•>-

-<●>-

My favorite city to visit is New Orleans. You can do things down there that would get you arrested back home.

-<●>-

I'm not a gifted writer. I have the clippings to prove it.

-<●>-

Your first job is the most important job because you can't make a comeback if you haven't done anything.

-<●>-

-<●>-

In the old days we made people walk the plank or put them in stocks. Today we make them conduct a press conference.

-<●>-

I took a wrong turn in a road race once. I knew something was wrong right after I ran through a creek.

-<●>-

-<•>-

I have a guaranteed cure for writer's block. I think of my mortgage payment, car payments and credit card charges. I don't get paid unless I write. It's amazing how quickly the creative juices start to flow.

-<•>-

The first thing I learned about talk radio is that an hour goes by in what seems like a few minutes or in what seems like a few days. It depends on how many calls you are getting.

-<•>-

There's only one way to learn about making a speech, only one way to get comfortable behind a podium in front of a crowd. You have to do it, and not just a few times. You have to do it over and over and over. After five years it gets easier.

-<●>-

We had a new reporter at the Observer-Dispatch, a nice young guy. He didn't really want to be a journalist, though. He wanted to be a musician.

Maybe he had his mind on music the night he went to cover a meeting of the Yorkville Village Board.

Yorkville is a small village. The meetings are short and easy to cover. So it was not unusual to see the reporter return early from the meeting. But he was back very early. His feet were up on the desk and he was reading the newspaper.

"What happened?" I asked, figuring the meeting must have been even shorter than usual and that he had written a very quick story.

"There wasn't anything to write about," he said. "There wasn't even a meeting."

"Oh?"

"It got canceled. The mayor died on the way to the meeting."

The reporter left the O-D not long after that. I don't know what happened to him, but I hope he is playing an instrument somewhere and having a good time.

-<>-

-<●>-

No matter in which direction you are biking, the wind is always in your face, you are always going uphill, and the shade is on the other side of the road.

-<●>-

The highest paid editors call the most meetings. The lowest paid reporters do the most work and don't get weekends off.

-<●>-

There are only two kinds of people in this world, those who think O.J. is guilty and those who think he got framed.

-<●>-

If restaurants or entertainers are advertised as "famous," they aren't.

-<●>-

When the speaker says "in closing" or "let me conclude by saying," it means there are five more minutes in the speech.

-<●>-

When several people share a cab, the passenger in the front seat always gets stuck paying the fare.

-<●>-

If all the cars are headed west and you are in the only one going east, you are either going the wrong way on a one way street or something very interesting is happening somewhere west of you.

-<●>-

I admit I write a simple column. That's because most of us are simple people.

-<●>-

I have a perfect face for radio.

-<●>-

To be a good reporter you need the ability not to quote exactly what people say but rather to paraphrase what it is they really mean.

-<●>-

Always think twice before asking a woman whether she's pregnant. Never ask by who.

-<●>-

Some politicians are about as useful as a parachute on a plane that never leaves the ground.

-<●>-

Running the Boilermaker is like sex. When it's good, it's very very good. And when it's bad, it's still pretty good.

-<●>-

No matter how good something is, a good newspaper will find something bad.

-<●>-

An editorial writer is like a man with 20-20 eyesight riding backward on a train. He sees everything, but only after it has gone by.

I have hidden talents, so well hidden not even I can find them.

There are days when people say hello to me and I'm stuck for an answer.

I hate to brag but I've always been smart. Hell, I was the first kid in my class to learn his ABD's.

-<●>-

-<●>-

If I daydream enough at work, sooner or later one of those dreams will come true and I'll be outta here.

-<●>-

-<●>-

On the second Sunday in July, everybody would like to be running the Boilermaker. The problem is that only a few of them are willing to put in the months of training that takes.

-<●>-

The Boilermaker is already the best 15-K road race in the country. There will come a day when it's also the biggest in the country, and that day isn't too far off.

-<●>-

Without spectators lining the course, the Boilermaker would be just another road race.

-<●>-

-<●>-

The following story was told to me by an attorney. He swears it actually happened.

An 81-year-old woman walked into a lawyer's office and said she wanted to file for a divorce.

"How long have you been married?" asked the lawyer.

"It will be 61 years."

"Why," asked the lawyer, "would you want to get divorced now?"

"Enough is enough."

-<●>-

-<●>-

The best advice anybody ever gave me was to never give anybody any advice. And as a rule I don't give advice. There are, however, exceptions to every rule.

This is one of those times. Here is some advice:

• Never shoot pool with someone who arrives with their own cue stick.

• Never get on an airplane with any kind of drips coming out of it.

• Never drink before noon, except on St. Patrick's Day, in Cooperstown at the Hall of Fame game and on Boilermaker Sunday.

• Never eat where truck drivers eat. They don't care what they put in their stomachs.

- Never anger a waiter, a waitress, a chef or anybody else in the kitchen until after they have handed over your food.

- Never eat in restaurants with a dirty floor, dirty windows or dirty bathrooms.

- Never let people borrow books, video tapes or CDs. You'll never get them back. That's how I started my collection of books, tapes and CDs.

- Never try to teach your spouse how to drive a car with standard transmission or how to hit a golf ball.

- Never fly on an airline with a crew that speaks English as a second language.

-<>-

Everybody looks like a dork when wearing a bicycle helmet.

-<●>-

-<●>-

On my way to the radio station to do my show, I always stop at Holland Farms for a cup of coffee and a powdered sugar jelly bun, which I drink and eat while on the air. It's one of the reasons I'm doing a talk show on radio and not on TV.

-<●>-

There are more good jokes told about golf than any other sport. The fewest jokes are told about badminton. Why this is I don't know.

-<●>-

-<●>-

These are excerpts from letters I've received and messages left on my answering machine:

Dear Mr. Kelly:
I was surprised to read in your "things I didn't know" column the other day that you didn't know the rose was the state flower. Where have you been? - R. P.

Dear R. P.:
In my backyard, which is why I thought the state flower was the dandelion.

-<●>-

Dear Mr. Kelly:
I look forward to reading your column and was worried when it wasn't in the paper Wednesday or Friday. Vacation? - L. E.

Dear L. E.:
Thanks for caring. I was temporarily transferred to the newspaper's Brookfield bureau after some fink wrote and told my boss I didn't know the name of the state flower.

Dear Mr. Kelly:
As a rule we enjoy your column. The column you wrote about modern art proves once again that there's an exception to every rule. - Unsigned

Dear Unsigned:
The people who send me letters are intelligent and polite. But as you pointed out, there are exceptions to every rule.

Dear Mr. Kelly:
Trying to compare your schedule with Donald Trump's schedule is preposterous. - Unsigned

Dear Unsigned:
That was supposed to be the idea.

-<●>-

Dear Mr. Kelly:
You are probably sick of people writing to you about Kewpees, but I just had to tell you what a wonderful story you did. It brought back many memories. But I find it difficult to believe the Kewpee hamburgers in Ohio are better than what we had at Utica's Kewpee. - D. E.

Dear D. E.:
There are several things in life I never tire of, praise and Kewpee hamburgers are two of them. Thanks for your kind words. As for your disbelief, maybe you're right. Maybe I should go back to Ohio and eat more Kewpee hamburgers just to be sure.

-<●>-

-<●>-

Dear Mr. Kelly:
I'm calling in regard to your article on Joe Angerosa, the man going to Las Vegas to play Elvis. This is probably a bizarre question, but I'd like to get in touch with him to see if he's having any kind of a moving sale on his old Elvis costumes. My brother is trying to break into the Elvis impersonation business in Japan in the fall. I'm trying to help out by buying him an older Elvis costume. - B. R.

Dear B. R.:
First off, let me get something straight. Are you trying to get in touch with Elvis or Joe Angerosa? If it's the former, your request is, to say the least, unusual. If it's the latter, it doesn't even begin to compare with some of the bizarre requests I get. Anyway, Joe isn't having a moving sale, but maybe somebody else out there has an old Elvis costume and will let me know.

-<●>-

-<●>-

Dear Mr. Kelly:
For someone who makes a profession out of being thin-skinned about off-hand commentary on Utica, you seem all too eager to be off-hand about other cities. Case in point: your gratuitous and unfounded remark about gourmet restaurants in Cincinnati as in the above referenced article. This isn't the first time you've dumped on Cincinnati for no apparent reason. I am a transplanted Yankee who has lived in Cincinnati. I can attest from first-hand knowledge that Cincinnati is not only a fine city, but a city of fine restaurants. So I don't understand your "gourmet restaurant" insult. - W. K.

Dear W. K.:
It's easy to explain. My computer has a short in its wiring and when I write Pittsburgh it comes out Cincinnati. By the way, the way to spot a gourmet restaurant in Cincinnati (actually typed Pittsburgh) is to look for a golden arch.

-<●>-

-<●>-

Dear Mr. Kelly:
While reading your column in today's paper, I was surprised by something you wrote. The article on Charles Kuralt's favorite places and your favorite places was great reading until I came upon the final paragraph. You had a great piece of writing and then you killed it by ending on such a negative note. In the future, I suggest you stay away from negativity in your columns. - G. Z.

Dear G. Z.:
Are you a writer? Probably. You picked right up on a major flaw in my style. I'm positive and upbeat until the very last line of whatever it is I'm writing and then something comes over me and I get negative. Anyway, thanks for the really great letter. It was nice of you to take the time to write. I enjoy getting stupid letters.

-<●>-

-<●>-

Dear Mr. Kelly:
In a recent column you wrote, "If you're playing Scrabble with me, better come armed with an unabridged dictionary." If you really were an excellent Scrabble player, you would know that it is against the rules to use an unabridged dictionary. - L. O.

Dear L. O.:
When you play Scrabble with me, you play by my rules and unabridged dictionaries are allowed. Also permitted are Pakistani and Iraqi dictionaries. That's how I manage to win games using words such as "qxiyz" and "xzkloopzq."

-<●>-

Dear Mr. Kelly:
A column about men's pockets is fine, but if you really want to see something, poke around in a woman's purse sometime. - L.

Dear L.:
I once did. She slapped me.

Dear Mr. Kelly:
Go back to your old picture. The face on the new one is faded out. - Unsigned

Dear Unsigned:
That's what happens when you have been writing a column for as long as I have.

Dear Mr. Kelly:
The column about Miss McCalmont was one of your best ever. She taught me Palmer Method and she taught my children. She is a great lady. Thanks for letting us know she is alive and well. I intend to write her. - B. L.

Dear B. L.:
If you write, make sure to use Palmer Method. Practice by doing push-pulls and ovals. And as Miss McCalmont would say, "place your wrist flat on the desk and glide, glide, glide."

-<•>-

Dear Mr. Kelly:
Miss McCalmont was as good as they get and as tough as they get. That's why she is so well remembered. - P. T.

Dear P. T.:
And that's why she has always been so well respected.

Dear Mr. Kelly:
I find it difficult to read some - although not all - of your columns without throwing up. - Unsigned
P.S. - The number of your columns that make me sick outnumber the ones that don't.

Dear Unsigned:
I know exactly what you mean. While writing some - although not all - of my columns, I find that taking Kaopectate can be very effective.
P.S. - If I ever need a brain transplant, I'll ask for yours. I want one that hasn't been used.

Dear Mr. Kelly:
Newspapers have gone way overboard with the Elvis stamp. Do you think people are interested in such nonsense? - Unsigned

Dear Unsigned:
Nope. I just write things about Elvis so that people will get mad at me. My day isn't complete until someone calls me a jerk.

Dear Mr. Kelly:
In response to your column, "Kelly's Laws," in today's paper you said the amount of stress an executive is under can be measured by taking the number of paper clips he or she has strung together in one hour and multiplying by the person's age. My response: Who the heck has time to sit and string paper clips???" - S. O.

Dear S. O.:
First off, calm down. You are so stressed out i t is affecting your punctuation. Secondly, if you are going to be a regular reader of my column, you'd better get in a good supply of Kaopectate.

Dear Mr. Kelly:
This is a fan letter. I read the comics, the obituaries, Ann Landers, Mike Royko and Joe Kelly. All of them give me great pleasure. Thank you. - S. S

Dear S. S:
Thank you. I have two questions, though. 1. Do you read those things in that order? 2. Since reading obituaries gives you "great pleasure," do you mind if I ask what line of work you're in?

Dear Mr. Kelly:
How could you claim to be an Elvis fan and then write garbage about him? Talk about being two faced. - Male voice on answering machine.

Dear Sir:
If I had two faces do you think I'd use the one appearing with this column?

Dear Mr. Kelly:
Loved the column about the New York, Susquehanna and Western Railway's steam engine. What a thrill it must have been for you to ride in the engine. Hope you'll do more columns on the railway. I was one of those people lining the track as the engine came into Utica. - G. H.

Dear G. H.:
I thought all those people lining the track were there to see me in my engineer's hat. Are you claiming they were there to see a steam engine?

Dear Mr. Kelly:
I take exception to your remark that Elvis was "fat as a pig." Writing something like that is uncalled for and inaccurate. I think Elvis deserves to be placed on a stamp. - A.C.

Dear A. C.:
You're right. I was callous. Worse, I was inaccurate. I should have said Elvis was fat as a cow.

Dear Mr. Kelly:
I've got a complaint. Because of all the columns you wrote about America's Greatest Heart Run & Walk, I went out and ran five miles through wind, snow and cold. I had a great time. Now I'm thinking about running my first Boilermaker. - Female voice on answering machine.

Dear Lady:
Glad you had a great time at the Heart Run & Walk. I hope you aren't disappointed with the Boilermaker, though. It's never windy, snowy or cold.

-<●>-

Dear Mr. Kelly:
You're always making fun of (Mario) Cuomo. Why don't you make (Lou) LaPolla and (Ray) Meier look foolish for a change?-A. B.

Dear A. B.:
They don't need help from me.

Dear Mr. Kelly:
I was recently in Bangor, Maine, and saw Stephen King's house. I've been one of his fans for years and have been very interested in the columns you have written about him. You quoted Stephen King as saying he gets his ideas from Utica, NY. Where do you get your ideas? - M. H.

Dear M. H. :
Bangor, Maine.

Dear Mr. Kelly:
Not long ago you wrote in the newspaper that you were 23 years old. My mother says you were kidding. Were you? - L. M.

Dear L. M.:
Your mother is correct. I was kidding. I'm 22.

Dear Mr. Kelly:
I never miss reading your column. You make me laugh and you make me cry. Please don't ever stop. I only wish you had a column in the newspaper every day. - M. T.

Dear M. T.:
Thanks for your nice letter. I hope you'll write again. If you do, please send copies of your letters to the management of the Observer-Dispatch. Their names can be found in a little box on the bottom of the editorial page. Just don't mention anything about me writing seven columns a week.

Dear Mr. Kelly:
Thank you for speaking to our club. The ladies enjoyed it. You don't look at all like your picture. - L. E.

Dear L. E.:
I look exactly like myself. I don't know who was speaking to your club, but it wasn't me. I was stuck in traffic in Boonville that night.

-<●>-

Dear Mr. Kelly:
Our journalism class from New Hartford High School toured the newspaper. It was very nice of you to take time and talk to our class. - S. J.

Dear S. J.:
It must be that impostor again. I am rarely in the office and on those few occasions when I am forced to be there, I'm grouchy.

Dear Mr. Kelly:
Re your column on "99 things a man should do by the time he is 30," grow up!!! - P. M.

Dear P. M.:
I have two things to say. One, anyone who uses three exclamation points when a period will do is excitable and subject to high blood pressure. Two, I don't want to grow up. If I did, they wouldn't let me be a columnist anymore.

Dear Mr. Kelly:
Why don't you let up on smokers? We are people, too. We're just like everybody else. - A. K.

Dear A. K.:
Then how come they make you sit in a special section in restaurants?

Dear Mr. Kelly:
I've enclosed a clipping of your column and have circled a grammatical error. I am not an English teacher, but I think you ought to set a better example for our young people. - B. D.

Dear B. D.:
I went back and checked that column. You are wrong. There was not ONE mistake in grammar. There were TWO mistakes. The fellow who checks my columns for grammar, a nice man who supports an invalid wife, four kids and a mother-in-law, failed to catch the mistakes. He has been fired. Thanks for bringing the matter to our attention. Have a nice day.

Dear Mr. Kelly:
I most always enjoy your columns, but I did not like your column on Oral Roberts. - M. C.

Dear M. C.:
I didn't like it either. That one must have been written by Dave Dudajek.

Dear Mr. Kelly:
I've been enjoying your columns about Utica Free Academy. It was a great school with a great tradition. Its closing makes me very sad. - E. M.

Dear E. M.:
Me, too. And judging from the mail I've received, we've got lots of company.

Dear Mr. Kelly:
Enough already about UFA. Most of us could care less. UFA is dead. Write about something else. - Proctor, Class of '62.

Dear Proctor:
Thanks for the sympathy. I'll bet you provide great comfort at wakes.

Dear Mr. Kelly:
Two of your "You are getting old if you remember when" columns are hanging from my refrigerator. They are turning yellow. How about a new one? - L. J.

Dear L. J.:
Thank you. Being hung from a refrigerator is the highest compliment one can pay a columnist. By the way, if you keep clippings in the refrigerator instead of on the refrigerator, they won't yellow so quickly.

-<>-

Dear Mr. Kelly:
Every now and then, you slip a snide remark about Syracuse into your column. But if you were to be honest, you'd have to say that Syracuse has more to offer than Utica. - M. B.

Dear M. B.:
If I were to be honest, I'd say that I wish people who prefer Syracuse to Utica would move there.

Dear Mr. Kelly:
I can tell from your writing that you are a warm and caring person, and you have a great sense of humor. - B. R.

Dear B. R.:
You've got the wrong person. Nobody at this newspaper fits that description.

Dear Mr. Kelly:
Your column about phobias was a bunch of nonsense. I can describe it in one word: stupid. - No name.

Dear No Name:
If you intend writing every time I write something stupid, you had better get a bulk rate permit from the Postal Service.

Dear Mr. Kelly:
The way you and your rag newspaper are covering this mayoral election is awful. You are all a bunch of perfect idiots. - Unsigned

Dear Unsigned:
No one is perfect.

Dear Mr. Kelly:
Your continuing support of the Utica Boilermaker is appreciated. I'm not a runner myself, but my son and his wife are. By the way, my son beat you in this year's race. - L. R.

Dear L. R.:
The Boilermaker is one of the things this community does right. By the way, tell your son to set his sights higher for next year's race. Beating me isn't much of an accomplishment.

Dear Mr. Kelly:
I really enjoyed your column on unusual city and town names. I thought you might be interested to know that in Pennsylvania the town of Intercourse is just north of Paradise. - S. W.

Dear S. W.:
Your assumption is correct. I am interested in Intercourse and Paradise.

Dear Mr. Kelly:
Your columns are a bright spot in my day. I especially like your columns on history, and I loved your columns from the train trip from around the country, and I agree 100 percent with what you said about the flag burning. I could go on and on. - M. R.

Dear M. R.:
I wish you would.

-<•>-

Dear Mr. Kelly:
Your wrote that Bushy Graham was welterweight champion of the world. He was not. He was a champion, but he was bantamweight champion. - P. L.

Dear P. L.:
At least I got it half right, which is better than I usually do.

Dear Mr. Kelly:
I wrote in opposition to your first column about the flag burning. You saw fit not to respond. This letter of opposition is in response to your second column about flag burning. I hope you'll have the courtesy to respond to this letter. - R.H.

Dear R. H.:
Your second letter was better than your first, but then it would have to be.

Dear Mr. Kelly:
I hope you don't think this is too personal of a question, but we long-time readers wonder why the picture of you that appears with your column hasn't changed in the past seven or eight years. - A. G.

Dear A. G.:
The reason is quite simple. I haven't aged.

Dear Mr. Kelly:
I should have written long ago to tell you how much my sister and I enjoy your articles. Of special enjoyment were your stories from around the United States. We felt we were with you. - S. B. and B. B.

Dear S. B. and B. B.:
Which explains why my train berth felt so cramped.

Dear Mr. Kelly:
My husband and I love the columns you've written about Uticas in various parts of the country. We've saved them all.   But you missed one. There's a Utica in Illinois.   Interested? - T. W.

Dear T. W.:
Yes, and I will try to get out there, just as I've gotten to Uticas in Michigan, Missouri and Nebraska.   I will   not rest until I have visited every Utica.   I'm just keeping my fingers crossed that there's a Utica in Hawaii.

-<>-

Dear Mr. Kelly:
I'd be interested in your predictions for this year's Boilermaker. - C. R.

Dear C. R.:
I won't win.

-<>-

Dear Mr. Kelly:
Your flag waving columns are nice for people who like simplistic thinking and clichés. I certainly don't. - D. R.

Dear D. R.:
Then maybe I shouldn't tell you that in addition to the flag, I love Mom and apple pie.

Dear Mr. Kelly:
Enjoyed the column about your new publisher. His responses to your questions were very funny. Did he really write them? - F. D.

Dear F. D.:
I confess to helping him some. I wrote all the really funny responses. He wrote the others.

Dear Mr. Kelly:
Change your newspaper picture, please. We've been looking at that same OLD picture five times a week for years. - P. W.

Dear P. W.:
How do you think I feel? I have to look at it every morning.

Dear Mr. Kelly:
Thanks to you and the Observer-Dispatch for your support of the Boilermaker. And thanks to the other sponsors of the race. If you hear a cheer when you cross the finish line, it's me. - B. K.

Dear B. K.:
Thanks for the kind words. But if you plan on waiting for me to cross the finish line, you had better bring a lawn chair and lunch because you are going to be there awhile.

Dear Mr. Kelly:
Loved your column about the "revised" list of birthstones. But you overlooked a couple. A doctor's birthstone is a gallstone. A soda manufacturer's is a limestone. - J. R.

Dear J. R.:
I also left out jewelers, whose birthstone is the gemstone, and morticians, whose birthstone is the gravestone.

-<●>-

Dear Mr. Kelly:
I think you are an excellent columnist, but then again, what do I know? - L. L.

Dear L. L.:
Probably not much. At least you are a good judge of columnists.

-<●>-

Dear Mr. Kelly:
I found your column in yesterday's Observer-Dispatch quite disturbing - specifically your response to the observant reader who called your attention to your grammatical lapse. It's unfortunate that you hold your readers in such low regard. Your response to the writer, "Drop dead," was insulting and sophomoric. And it's doubly unfortunate that a person in your profession displays such cavalier disregard for the English language. - L. S.

Dear L. S.:
Let me respond point by point to your letter:
1. My response to the observant reader was tongue in cheek. Taken in context, it even made people with a sense of humor laugh, something you might like to try.

2. I often do sophomoric things, which is why they let me write a column.

3. I hold my readers in the highest regard. Without them, I'd have to get a real job.

4. As for your charge that I'm "cavalier," I take exception. I've never been in the U.S. Army and don't even know how to ride a horse.

Dear Mr. Kelly:
Go back to the place where you were taught how to write and demand a refund.   You got shortchanged. - Unsigned

Dear Unsigned:
If a bird had your brain it would fly backwards.

-<●>-

Dear Mr. Kelly:
I am 88 years old and remember many things about Utica. Attached is a list of shops and restaurants from the early days. Please excuse my handwriting. - M. J. R.

Dear M. J. R.:
Thanks for the information. Please write again, and don't apologize for your writing.   I know people half your age who can't write at all.

-<●>-

-<•>-

Dear Mr. Kelly:
Why not write a column exposing this garbage collection mess? The politicians are ruining us. It used to be just the city was bad, but now the county has gone bad. Write something on the raises the politicians are giving themselves. You should attend a Board of Education meeting if you really want to get depressed. - Unsigned

Dear Unsigned:
Although we've never met, I'll bet you wear one of those yellow smiley face pins.

-<•>-

Dear Mr. Kelly:
Perhaps you wouldn't be so quick to make fun of the Utica Board of Education if you knew what they were up against. - B. D.

Dear B. D.:
Until just recently, it seemed like it was each other.

-<•>-

Dear Mr. Kelly:
I heard you on the radio and it sounded like you had a cold. Next time you feel a cold coming on, try eating a little bit of garlic. It works. - L. L.

Dear L. L.:
There's no such thing as a little bit of garlic. By the way, I didn't have a cold. I always sound that way.

-<•>-

-<●>-

Dear Mr. Kelly:
Enjoy your columns, especially your monthly mailbag columns. But you ought to be careful referring to some of the people who write to you as "stupid." - A Friend

Dear Friend:
I didn't know it was a secret.

-<●>-

Dear Mr. Kelly:
How much does the Observer-Dispatch pay you for putting such drivel in the paper? - Unsigned

Dear Unsigned:
They don't pay me anything. I pay them. Isn't that the way it works?

-<●>-

-<●>-

Dear Mr. Kelly:
I enjoyed your Christmas poem. - S. W.

Dear S. W.:
Counting me, I'd guess that makes a total of two of us.

-<●>-

Dear Mr. Kelly:
I've never written a fan letter before so I'm probably not doing this right, but I wanted to tell you that your column is a hit in my house. - L. E.

Dear L. E.:
Thanks for the kind words. Maybe I should get paid for doing this.

-<●>-

-<●>-

Dear Mr. Kelly:
I've noticed the little jabs you and Dave Dudajek exchange from time to time. Is that for real or just a put on?-L. S.

Dear L. S.:
Dave who?

-<●>-

I'm good at giving after dinner speeches because I know the secret to a good one: Offend no one, make everyone laugh at least three times and get them back out to the bar as quickly as possible.

-<●>-

When everybody agrees with me is when I start doubting myself.

-<●>-

The United States is the only country where the minority gets treated as if they were the majority. In large part, that's because of the way the news media handles the news.

-<●>-

I wish people weren't so concerned with being called Irish-American, Italian-American, African-American and all the rest. American should be enough.

-<●>-

I never miss the chance to vote. If you don't vote you can't bitch about the people who get elected.

-<●>-

Sometimes people in our area have a way of making things sound even worse than they are.

-<●>-

If it can be written in simple English, it can be simply misunderstood.

-<●>-

On Dave Dudajek:
We've been friends for years. I got him started running and even gave him his first pair of running shoes. Now he beats me in races. That's how he shows his gratitude.

-<●>-

There were days as a reporter when going to work made me feel like I was part of a circular firing squad.

-<●>-

This area's best and brightest are too good and too smart to run for office. That's why we have the problems we do.

-<●>-

Saying "no comment" to a reporter makes it sound like you have something to hide, even if you don't. Saying "no comment" isn't very smart.

-<●>-

-<●>-

If there's one piece of advice I'd give to someone coming on my radio show for the first time, this would be it: We'll be on the air for an hour. Make sure you go to the bathroom before the show starts.

-<●>-

One of the things I've learned as a talk show host is that some people enjoy beating a dead horse to death.

-<●>-

None of the really good politicians lie unless it is absolutely necessary.

-<●>-

The good reporters get comments from both sides. That's how you get a public fight going and that's how you get a good story.

-<●>-

-<●>-

You can tell how badly someone wants a job at City Hall by how hard they work as a volunteer during the mayoral campaign.

-<●>-

On the Observer-Dispatch:
My first day on the job was in 1976 and I learned something that day from managing editor Tony Vella. He called me into his office, took a drag on an unfiltered cigarette and said, "You make me look good and I'll make you look good." I did and so did he.

-<●>-

There is no such thing as a deadline. There is always a minute or two more.

-<●>-

-<●>-

People who frequently stop at garage sales tend to have houses that look like garages.

-<●>-

Computers are getting more and more like humans. One of these days a computer will make a mistake and it will place the blame on another computer.

-<●>-

Police arrested several hookers and brought them into court. The judge spoke to the first hooker.

"Are you a prostitute?"

"I was only out for a walk, your honor. I'm a secretary."

The second woman responded that she wasn't a prostitute, either. She claimed to be a secretary out walking the streets to get exercise.

Four other hookers in the police roundup also denied being prostitutes. Each claimed to be a secretary.

The last woman in the bunch stood before the judge.

"Well," said the judge, "what do you do for a living?"

"I'm a hooker," she responded.

"How's business?" asked the judge.

"It would be great if all these damn secretaries weren't out there."

-<●>-

Old accountants never die, they just lose their balance.

———

Old mailmen never die, they just lost their zip.

———

Old doctors never die, they just lose their patients.

———

Old anesthetists never die, they just lose their feelings.

———

Old bankers never die, they just lose their cents.

———

Old investors never die, they just lose their interest.

———

Old barbers never die, they just lose their hair.

Old gamblers never die, they just lose their shirts.

Old navigators never die, they just lose their way.

Old lawyers never die, they just lose their briefs.

Old teachers never die, they just lose their class.

Old fishermen never die, they just smell that way.

-<●>-

A suspicious-looking man drove up to the border crossing.

"What's in the sacks?" the border patrol officer asked as he pointed to five large canvas bags on the back seat.

"Dirt," said the driver, "nothing but dirt."

"Take the bags out of the car," ordered the officer. "We'll have to inspect them."

The contents of each bag were poured out. All the officer could find was dirt. Although he was sure the man was smuggling something, the officer had no choice but to pass him through customs.

A week later the same suspicious-looking man drove up to the same border crossing. The same officer was on duty.

"What's in the bags this time?" asked the officer as he looked at 10 canvas sacks on the back seat.

"Dirt, officer, nothing but dirt."

Once again the officer searched the bags for contraband. All he found was dirt. The suspicious-looking man was again allowed to cross the border.

The same thing happened every week for the next year. Each time the sacks were inspected. Each time nothing except dirt was found. The frustrated officer even had the dirt analyzed. It was dirt, nothing but dirt.

Finally, out of frustration, the border crossing guard quit his job and became a bartender.

Several months later, just by chance, the suspicious-looking guy walked into the bar where the ex-border guard was working. The ex-officer recognized him at once.

"Listen, pal, your drinks are on the house all night if you'll just tell me one thing. I know you were up to no good. What were you smuggling?"

The suspicious-looking man looked around to make sure no one was listening, leaned over the bar and whispered - "Cars."

-<●>-

As a rule it takes me five to six hours to write a column that looks as if it was written in 15 or 20 minutes.

-<●>-

I'm doing everything I can to help the F. X. Matt Brewing Company increase sales.

-<●>-

The nicest trips are those with no fixed route and no dates of arrival.

-<●>-

Coming up with ideas for five columns a week isn't all that difficult. When I'm having trouble I just bang my head against a hard wall for 30 minutes or so.

On giving a speech:
Oftentimes, when the audience applauds loudly and enthusiastically, it isn't because of what you've said. It's because you are finished saying it.

-<●>-

The only person who doesn't believe the speech is too long is the person delivering it.

-<●>-

If I've got something good to write, something that really interests me, I can write it standing up in a crowded elevator. And should a high school marching band get on at the next floor I'd pause to look, but only for a second.

-<●>-

-<●>-

There's an easy way to tell if you're a real writer. Try to stop writing. If you can, you aren't.

-<●>-

Writer's block means you haven't done anything, thus there is nothing to write about. The best cure for writer's block is to get out of the office and do something.

-<●>-

People who hold up signs on street corners stating they'll work for food seldom do. Cash is what they are looking for.

-<●>-

-<●>-

Writing a book is a lot like running a marathon. You began training for a marathon by running a mile. Then, mile by mile, you gradually build up to the point where you can run 26.2 miles. With a book, it's one page after another until you're finished.

-<●>-

The second worst thing in the world is standing in a book store with a stack of your freshly printed books on a table in front of you and watching people walk past without buying any. The worst thing is having people stop at the table, leaf through your book and then decide not to buy.

-<●>-

Being a writer isn't easy, but then neither is being a janitor or an architect. Work is work.

-<●>-

Writing is simple but it isn't very easy.

-<●>-

Whether it's a newspaper column, book, short story, letter or memo, writing isn't fun. Anybody who says it is doesn't write for a living.

-<●>-

The more you write the better it should get. If that doesn't happen, you may want to see about getting a real estate license.

-<●>-

Good writers should write. Bad writers should become lawyers or plumbers, but they shouldn't become editors or critics, which, unfortunately, tends to happen.

-<●>-

I type with two fingers, not because I don't know how to type with the others but because my mind doesn't work fast enough to keep pace if I use all of them.

-<●>-

The good part about being a full-time newspaper columnist is that everything I hear or see is something I consider for a column. The bad thing about being a full-time columnist is that everything I hear or see is something I consider for a column.

-<●>-

-<•>-

The back door to the Observer-Dispatch building is on Catherine Street. That door was originally the front door. The front door of the Observer-Dispatch building is on Oriskany Street. That door was originally the back door. Maybe that's why I get confused whenever I enter the building.

-<•>-

The Observer-Dispatch newsroom is smoke free, quiet, color coordinated, nicely carpeted and nobody swears out loud, which is exactly opposite of the way it was when I started there in 1976.

-<•>-

-<•>-

I get a lot of work done while flying. The only people who bother you are the flight attendants, and then only to see whether you are hungry or thirsty, or to tell you to put your seatbelt on.

-<•>-

If I had known I was going to become a newspaper writer, I'd have paid a lot more attention when I was in school. And I certainly wouldn't have skipped school so much.

-<•>-

Newspaper writers have bigger egos than newspaper editors. That's why they write instead of edit.

-<•>-

-<●>-

I am 6 feet, 9 inches tall, although I look shorter than that in my newspaper picture. It has something to do with the brand of film our photographers use.

Writing is never easy, but there are times when it seems nearly impossible. On those days I admit defeat and go for a run.

-<•>-

Never say what you've written is bad. People might think it's good. There's no explaining some people's taste.

-<•>-

For a college student to say, "I want my first newspaper job to be that of a columnist" is like a baseball player saying he's going to steal second before he gets to first.

-<•>-

When I started at the Observer-Dispatch, I didn't have gray hair, didn't wear glasses, was skinny and didn't drink. That should tell you something about what writing does to you.

A good radio talk show guest knows never to shake their head or shrug their shoulders when answering a question. They also know to keep talking if the host is in the process of taking a drink from his cup of coffee or eating a jelly bun.

-<●>-

The Observer-Dispatch is a great institution, but then it would have to be to survive some of the people who have worked here.

-<•>-

I worked at (Utica's) City Hall in the early 1970s. I learned many things while working there. Given enough time I'll think of one.

-<•>-

The best stories are usually the ones the reporters tell each other in the barroom after work.

-<•>-

If you are at a fire, accident, press conference, parade or anything else, decide what's the first thing you'd tell a friend who hadn't been there. That's your lead.

-<●>-

There's nothing complicated about writing a news article. You go somewhere, see what's happening, return to the newsroom and type the story, starting with the most important thing.

-<●>-

Many of the reporters I've worked with have been arrogant. The best of them have been the most arrogant.

-<●>-

-<●>-

Mike and John were unloading their golf clubs from the trunk of their car. Just then a long funeral procession went past.

Mike adjusted the clubs in his bag while John stopped what he was doing, removed his golf hat, placed it over his heart and bowed his head in prayer.

"I have to tell you something, John. That was one of the nicest and most thoughtful things I've ever seen you do."

"It was the least I could do," John said. "Today would have been our 40th wedding anniversary."

-<●>-

-<●>-

The difference between a professional writer and an amateur is that the professional writes no matter what else is happening in the world, no matter what else is happening in his or her own personal life, and no matter how difficult the working conditions. The amateur, though, has to have everything just right to be able to write.

-<●>-

There are good writing days and bad writing days, and then there are days when I have trouble writing my byline.

-<●>-

Me telling other people how to write is like Gen. Custer at the Battle of the Little Big Horn telling his men to take no prisoners.

-<●>-

Journalists are a complaining bunch, and it's tolerated by management. It's a perk enjoyed by journalists the world over. It's what we get instead of a big salary.

Which reminds me of a monk. He joined a monastery where speaking was permitted only once every 10 years and even then only three words were allowed.

After his first 10 years the monk was called into the chief monk's office and given permission to speak his three words.

"Food is rotten," the monk said.

He then returned to the fields, where he worked from sunrise to sunset, week in and week out, month after month.

Ten years later he returned to the office and again was given permission to speak three words.

"Bed is hard."

Ten more years of back breaking work followed. Then it was back to the chief monk's office to speak three words.

"Room is cold," said the monk.

Back to the fields he headed. This time, though, he turned around and went back to the head monk's office.

"I can't take it anymore," said the monk. "I quit."

"I'm not surprised," said the chief monk. "All you've done since you've been here is bitch, bitch, bitch."

-<●>-

It's easy to tell when it's black fly season in the Adirondacks. Women up there wear insect repellent instead of perfume.

-<●>-

The good news is that I now have an hour-long talk show on WIBX. The bad news is the same thing.

-<●>-

There's nothing wrong with good politics and smart politicians. The problem in Utica is that we've had bad politics and too many stupid politicians.

-<●>-

If there's one place in the United States where you have to pace your drinking it's New Orleans. If you get carried away down there, you won't remember being there.

There are places in New Orleans where you can't be sure if the female entertainers are men pretending to be women or vice versa.

-<●>-

I've been in some interesting places in New Orleans. I wouldn't want to tell my mother about them, though.

-<●>-

If I waited for inspiration, I'd never write anything.

-<●>-

Writing the first thing in the morning is the best way I know of ruining a perfectly good day.

-<●>-

I'm pretty good at keeping secrets. It's the blabbermouths I tell who spill the beans.

-<●>-

It's easier to write serious stuff than it is to write funny stuff. That's because there are more people on the verge of tears than on the verge of laughter. It's also because writers are usually in a state of gloom, sometimes even despair.

Getting a book printed is easy. Selling them is the tough part.

The best editors convince the worst writers that they have talent. Then those editors show those writers how to change things.

You'll never go wrong by putting a period after a short sentence.

-<●>-

There are times when I know how I will end the column before I know how it will begin. When that happens, the column is usually a good one.

-<●>-

The more I rewrite something, the shorter i t gets. That's usually a good thing.

-<●>-

To make a point or to rally people to your cause, it is necessary to pound away at it day after day. Write about it once and people will shrug their shoulders and say, "That's true" and then move on to something else. Only by making your point over and over does the message begin to sink in.

There are four instances when it's easy to think about your writing: while driving a car, while running, while in the shower and while sitting alone at a bar with a drink in your hand. Unfortunately, it isn't easy to actually write while doing any of those things.

Best selling books have been written while the authors have been in prison. A convict once told me prison was a good place to write. Somebody else prepares meals and takes out the garbage. The telephone doesn't ring and nobody ever drops by to say hello. And there's no temptation to stop writing to go have a couple beers.

I have a tough time writing when the sun is shining on a beautiful day. Now that I think about it, it's just as tough when it's raining.

-<>-

People have told me to stop acting like a jerk. I wish I was acting.

-<>-

-<●>-

Writing a newspaper column, a radio script or a book isn't the easiest thing in the world, but it isn't brain surgery.

-<●>-

When someone asks you to give an honest appraisal of what they've written, they really don't want an honest appraisal. Nobody wants to hear they should give up writing and take up plumbing. What people really want is encouragement and praise, two things writers don't often get.

-<●>-

Writers are some of the most insecure people in the world. I think that's why so many of them become drunks.

Saying you're a writer is a good way to attract the attention of the opposite sex. The trouble is that somewhere down the line you have to produce evidence that you are what you say you are.

If writers wrote like they talked, most of them would immediately improve.

I usually find that if I enjoy something I've written, other people do too.

Paul Harvey has it right. Listen to what someone tells you, but always make sure to get "the rest of the story."

-<●>-

If the mind listened to the body, people would never get up in the morning or run a marathon.

When I was a kid I went to the movies every Saturday. Back then, X and R were just letters of the alphabet.

Word processors and high speed printers make it possible for anybody to easily turn out their writing. That's too bad.

Radar is radar spelled backwards.

-<●>-

Finish a marathon and you can finish anything.

-<●>-

We don't need a comedy club in Utica. We've got politics.

-<●>-

When Murphy said, "Anything that can go wrong will go wrong," he was riding Amtrak.

-<●>-

Never buy a big suitcase. You'll always fill it.

-<●>-

The best travelers are the ones who keep on moving.

-<●>-

A trip doesn't always have to have a destination.

-<●>-

The best way to find out if you like someone is to go on a long trip with them.

-<●>-

Expect things to go wrong when you travel. You'll never be disappointed.

People in too much of a hurry to get where they are going sometimes miss the best part of their vacation.

-<●>-

The best travelers have the most understanding and the most patience.

-<●>-

One of the lonliest sounds in the world is the whistle of a train going through a crossing at night.

-<●>-

There are two kinds of people in this world, people who love to travel and everybody else.

If you want to experience sadness, start a train trip at night, in a soft rain, kissing someone good-bye on a train platform.

-<●>-

I'm lucky. I like to travel just because I like to travel.

-<●>-

When boarding an airliner, always make sure to check the people sitting in first class. You can't ever be sure who you'll see there. So far I've seen Larry King, Chubby Checker and Peter Jennings. I hope to do better, though.

-<●>-

-<●>-

Traveling is lonely only when you don't have a home to return to.

-<●>-

The best way to get something to write about is to travel.

-<●>-

Amtrak bathrooms and Amtrak windows have something in common. They're never clean.

-<●>-

On journalism students:
I tell all of them the same thing: "Go to medical school."

If editorial writers were as smart as they think they are, they'd be doing something else for a living.

I make it a point never to read Letters to the Editor. If someone writes something good about me, I might believe it. If they write something bad, I'll get mad.

When I'm out of town the first thing I do is pick up the newspaper and read Letters to the Editor. It's the most interesting part of any newspaper.

-<●>-

One of the nice things about train travel is speeding through midwestern towns and looking into the windows of houses near the tracks and using your imagination as to what's going on inside.

-<●>-

When I'm home I can't wait to get on the road. When I'm a long way from home, I can't wait to get back. A few days at home and I'm ready to hit the road again.

-<●>-

Always pack aspirin, a safety pin, a Swiss Army knife, map and a good book. At one point or another in your trip, you'll use all five. Sometimes you'll use them more than once. Sometimes you'll use them all at once.

-<●>-

To travel long distances by bicycle is a wonderful way to see the country. You can smell the aroma of things being cooked. You can say hello to people and wave, all without stopping. You had better be in good shape, though.

-<●>-

I know how to get around in New York City better than many of the people driving cabs, and I don't know the city all that well.

-<●>-

On my first trip to the Grand Canyon I didn't see much. I was too busy taking pictures.

Years ago I interviewed a couple on the eve of their 60th wedding anniversary. They were a cute couple, sitting there holding hands.

I waited until the end of the interview to ask the obvious and most important question.

"To what do you attribute the secret of your long and successful marriage?" I inquired.

Without hesitation, she said, "Twice a week we take time to go out to a romantic dinner with candlelight, soft music, and dancing."

She paused and smiled before continuing.

"He goes on Tuesdays, I go on Thursdays."

-<●>-

Add them all up and six people are running for mayor this year. Take heart. Only one of them can win.

-<●>-

I love talking about the good old days, but I wouldn't want to live through them again.

-<●>-

I don't like getting into debates because there's a good chance I'll be proven wrong.

-<●>-

One thing I've learned from being a talk show host is that callers are united in their belief that the world is beset with problems. They are divided, though, on how to solve them.

-<●>-

On U.S. Senator Daniel Patrick Moynihan:
He has two faces and neither one is
pleasant to look at.

-<●>-

-<●>-

Never argue with your boss. You can't expect him or her to be as perfect as you.

-<●>-

Once, on the island of St. Thomas, while using a bathroom in a bar, someone limbo danced under the door and into the stall next to mine. It was my first and last visit to that bar and to the island of St. Thomas.

-<●>-

Winning the lottery is easier than getting a table at the Uptown Grill on St. Patrick's Day.

JOE KELLY'S RULES FOR SURVIVING ON THE JOB
NO MATTER WHAT THAT JOB HAPPENS TO BE

- When something goes wrong, no matter what it happens to be, blame the computer.

- If blaming the computer doesn't work, blame an underling.

- If you're sure you can complete the project on Tuesday, tell your boss that Friday is the absolute earliest you can get it done. Then take off Wednesday to play golf and finish the project Thursday, a day early. Everybody is happy.

- Don't leave the room while your boss is in mid-sentence.

- When tempted to call in sick, remember Wally Pipp. Wally Pipp played for the New York Yankees. In fact, he was in the starting lineup. Then he got a migraine headache and asked for the day off. He got it. His replacement was a fellow named Lou Gehrig. Pipp never got back into the lineup. In fact, he never played another game in a Yankee uniform.

- When mad and tempted to quit, remember that you might not have the best job in the world, but it's better than being a boxing promoter.

- If you can't convince the boss, confuse the boss.

- When talking to your boss, always explain your solution in the simplest way possible. That way, your boss has a chance of understanding it.

-<●>-

-<●>-

I've got one word of advice for someone trying to decide whether to run for office in Utica: "Don't."

-<●>-

Never eat at a place where more than six 18-wheel tractor trailers are parked outside. The same is true of motorcycles.

-<●>-

Most problems can be overcome with time. The ones that can't can be overcome with time can be overcome with money. Any problem can be overcome with time and money.

-<●>-

Mario Cuomo and I have at least one thing in common. He doesn't listen to my talk show and I don't listen to his. The arrangement seems to be working.

There's an easy way to tell whether someone is from New York City or Upstate. People from the city say they stand "on line." Upstaters stand "in line."

I can't tell you my true age because my mother doesn't tell people hers.

-<●>-

I love living in Central New York and would never move away. But I want a place in Florida to visit in January, February and March.

-<●>-

An entertaining writing style is very important. It doesn't matter how much valuable information a writer crams into a story if it's a story nobody reads.

-<●>-

The chances of me receiving some sort of big time writing award are about the same as walking into a bar and seeing Woody Allen having a friendly drink with Mia Farrow. It's possible but not very likely.

-<●>-

The Wit & Wisdom of Joe Kelly

ABOUT
THE
AUTHOR

Joe Kelly started working at the Observer-Dispatch when he was 11 years old. He had a paper route with 125 customers. In 1976 he started writing for the O-D as a reporter. His column started in 1984. He has a talk show on radio station WIBX, and is assistant director of the Boilermaker Road Race.

ABOUT
THE
ILLUSTRATOR

A Mohawk Valley native, Randall Kimberly, studied at the Art Students League in New York City. A professional artist and illustrator for the past 15 years, his work consistently achieves recognition in both national and international exhibitions. To area residents he is more likely known as the creator of *Crumbs Along the Mohawk*, an editorial cartoon with a satirical view of life in the area which runs in every Sunday Observer Dispatch. He resides in Utica with his wife Linda.

The Wit & Wisdom of Joe Kelly